INSTITUTE OF FINE ARTS, NEW YORK UNIVERSITY

THE FIRST ANNUAL

Walter W. S. Cook Alumni Lecture

DELIVERED ON THE OCCASION OF

THE DEDICATION OF THE JAMES B. DUKE HOUSE

FEBRUARY 9, 1959

Giotto and Assisi

BY MILLARD MEISS

NEW YORK UNIVERSITY PRESS : 1960

IT IS AN HONOR to address you at this celebration, and I feel privileged to be able to convey in this way my gratitude to teachers to whom I owe my training, and my pleasure in the Institute's continued vitality. I suppose that as a speaker I should be able to face so learned an audience in a relaxed state of mind, for I am one of the oldest surviving alumni, and not much is ever expected of them.

I entered the Department of Fine Arts at New York University in the spring of 1928, and shortly thereafter I heard Professor Offner expound one of the famous, old, refractory art-historical problems that were then, and still are, given to graduate students to help them cut their teeth. All these problems present the same essential difficulty—determination of the early works of great, revolutionary artists. Only one of them—the relationship of Masolino and Masaccio—has in the meantime been solved, in the historian's sense of winning general agreement. The controversies over Hubert and Jan van Eyck, and the *Legend of St. Francis* in the Upper Church at Assisi, remain. You might feel that a wise critic would stay clear of such issues, trusting that the future would somehow provide new facts that would finally settle them. Perhaps you are right. But if this evening I attempt to outline a solution of one of these problems it is not just because an issue involving the early work of Giotto is especially important, nor because my proposal is new. The continued attempt to solve the problem is justified more, I believe, by the fact that every historian of the period actually has an opinion about the matter—he simply cannot escape having one—and the opinion he holds affects, even if unknowingly, his judgment of every other similar issue in early Italian art. This is true because our conception of artistic individuality is shaped to a considerable degree by analogy. The *Legend of St. Francis* differs greatly from the Arena Chapel frescoes and later paintings by Giotto in character and in artistic strength, so that the usual inclusion of it nowadays among the master's works has served to sustain a general critical expansionism. To formulate the principle simply, if Giotto can look so different at different times, so can Pietro Lorenzetti. The one momentous decision about Assisi has had its effect upon the enlargement of the *oeuvres* of *all* the better painters of the time.

There are not many students today who deny the *Legend of St. Francis* to Giotto. His authorship of these frescoes is assumed, though not always with confidence, in a vast literature on all aspects of Italian painting of the late Middle Ages that has increased at an astonishing rate in recent years. The few disbelievers are sustained by the conviction of Friedrich Rintelen and Richard Offner, who in 1939 published the most penetrating recent account of the stylistic difficulties created by such an attribution. Historians are of course given powerful inducements to conceive of a Giotto so variable that he could have produced both the *Legend* and the frescoes in the Arena Chapel in Padua. As early as 1312 to 1318 a Ferrarese chronicler stated that the great Florentine had worked in the church of St. Francis in Assisi. About 1450 the sculptor Ghiberti cited paintings by him there also, identifying them by a peculiarly vague and hence controversial phrase that may have been intended to refer to the *Legend*. Vasari, in any event, believed that it did, and from the time of the publication of the second edition of his *Lives* in 1568 until the rise of modern criticism in the nineteenth century, it was taken for granted that the fresco cycle was Giotto's work. General historical plausibility strongly supports this opinion. The burden of proof lies—or at least should lie—heavily upon those who deny the cycle to Giotto.

The burden must now in one sense be increased. The date given to the *Legend* has varied with the attribution. Rintelen, his followers, and some others judged that the frescoes were painted after the Arena Chapel, anywhere up to 1320 or even 1350. In recent years this view has become increasingly difficult to maintain. It is now possible to prove definitely that it is incorrect. A couple of years ago John White pointed to the great similarities of the *Stigmatization of St. Francis* in Giuliano da Rimini's altarpiece in the Gardner Museum in Boston to the one in the *Legend* (Figs. 1, 3). The enframing architecture in the altarpiece, too, is anticipated in the Upper Church. The panel, dated 1307, presupposes the fresco, he argued, and hence this one fresco, at least, must have been finished by 1307. Since, on the other hand, the correspondences were limited to just one figure and some arches it seemed difficult to exclude the possibility that both panel and fresco reflected another, lost composition.

There can be no doubt, however, that Mr. White was right and that Giuliano da Rimini was in Assisi. *St. Clare* in the altarpiece of 1307 is, I have recognized recently, a copy of the image of this saint in the St. Nicholas Chapel in the Lower Church (Figs. 6, 7). Any doubt that the saint in the altarpiece is the copy rather than the original is banished by the fact that she holds the lily in her left hand as a consequence of reversal. Giuliano was especially interested in the motive of the drapery held by a hand in front of the body, and he repeated it in other figures on the altarpiece. The painter of the fresco of *St. Clare* is the most advanced of the masters who worked in this chapel; his style is in fact Giottesque in the Paduan sense (Fig. 5). Giuliano learned from other frescoes in the Chapel, too, for his *Madonna*, while not a copy of the frescoed *Madonna*, obviously owes much to it (Figs. 8, 9). Sometime before painting this altarpiece of 1307 for Urbania (near Urbino) Giuliano apparently had studied in S. Francesco, making drawings of figures he admired, just like the anonymous Trecento master whose sheet of copies of figures in various parts of the church, including the St. Nicholas Chapel, is now in the Fogg Museum (Figs. 2, 4).

A little-known contemporary of Giuliano was, it is now clear, his companion in the study of the frescoes of S. Francesco. One of his panels, an altarpiece in Cesi (near Terni), bears the precious date 1308 (Fig. 10). The Madonna is a precise copy of the extraordinary Madonna in the *Obsequies of St. Francis*, where it stands on the rood-beam as a type of older, venerated image (Fig. 11). The two apostles on the lower right of the Cesi altarpiece, Thomas and Matthew, are very similar to the corresponding apostles in the St. Nicholas Chapel (Figs. 12, 13). In a hitherto unknown tabernacle that, in an article now in the press, I attribute to the Cesi Master, there are forms drawn from two other frescoes in the Upper Church.

From all this it is apparent that the frescoes of the St. Nicholas Chapel, usually dated about 1310–1315, were in existence already in early 1307. Inasmuch as one of the styles (Fig. 7) presupposes Paduan Giottesque, either the Arena Chapel or a lost work by Giotto in the same phase must have been under way by 1306. This is valuable evidence of chronology, because while it is generally assumed that the Arena Chapel was painted around 1305, documents and written sources actually permit a range from 1304 to 1313.

At least two of the scenes of the *Legend* on the south wall of the Church were thus in existence before 1307–1308. These are among the later frescoes in the cycle, and since the Arena Chapel was probably being painted in 1304–1306 the *Legend* cannot have been begun significantly later than the Chapel. Rintelen and all his followers, therefore, were wrong. The frescoes are the work, not of a retarded painter, but of a modernist, if not a pioneer.

Scholars who divide on problems such as the relationship of the Assisi and Padua cycles usually maintain that their adversaries are deficient in perception. Some eyes are no doubt much sharper than others, but divergent opinions are caused not only by what scholars see but by how they interpret what they see. The opponents of Giotto's authorship of the *Legend* have sometimes insisted—to select the simplest of examples—upon the difference of format of the single scenes in Assisi and Padua. One painter, these scholars say, would not have set for his stories two such different kinds of spaces (Figs. 14, 15). But others quickly reply, rightly I think, that we do not

4

know whether in this matter the painter had a free choice; perhaps both the height and the total number of scenes were predetermined. At this juncture some students turn, more profitably of course, to the fact that the proportionately higher field in Assisi is accompanied, outdoors, by a panoramic landscape, and indoors, by a crown of lofty buildings (Figs. 64, 66). Nothing comparable is visible in Padua (Figs. 63, 65). The St. Francis master was certainly not, however, driven to such fantasies of terrain and architecture by the exigencies of his format. Given a field of this shape, he might have made his figures larger, or made them seem larger by a kind of design that we shall discuss later. Evidently he wanted the sort of vista the vertical format permitted. This is the opinion of many students today, but then they divide once more on the significance of this fundamental artistic choice. Most of them have concluded that the exceptional differences are the consequence of an exceptional commission: whereas in Padua Giotto portrayed events of a remote time and a distant place and was guided by long-established conventions, in Assisi he was required to tell the story of a great religious leader who was native to the region and who had not long ago been buried in the very church to be decorated.

Even if, however, we grant the effectiveness at that time of such a special stimulus, and the painter's capacity to transform his style accordingly, the discussion seems not yet sufficiently searching. Why should the painter of the *Legend* have been relatively more concerned with the environment of the saint than with his emotional, moral, or religious life, matters which absorbed the illustrator of the lives of Christ and the Virgin at Padua? In the scene of St. Francis giving his mantle to a knight who had once been rich (one of the frescoes in the cycle considered most characteristic of Giotto), the interchange between the generous giver and the grateful receiver has to withstand an undertow all around it (Fig. 15). The head of the saint is exactly at the crossing of two great diagonals which run on towards the corners of the field. They attract our attention down through the mantle or up toward the fluent rocks, the waving trees, the coruscating hill-town, and the church. At the saint's left his handsome horse, filling almost half the foreground, draws our eyes down to the level of the feet to watch him in the unprofitable act of browsing on a rocky terrain. Lest we fail to descend, his movement is repeated by the fall of the gesticulating mantle at the right. This mustard-colored stuff, spread wide between the figures, almost drowns their looks and actions in its strident rhetoric.

In the Arena Chapel nothing, however beautiful or interesting in itself, is permitted to infringe upon the human situation. At the moment of expulsion from the temple, the aggressive priest and the childless Joachim, clinging to his lamb as though it were a son, are locked forever in an unmitigated encounter (Fig. 16). This violent rejection, represented in the right-hand side of the field, is followed in the next scene by Joachim's return to his sheepfold, which is enacted at the left (Fig. 14). The old man has just moved slowly and heavily into the space, while the shepherds and their flock have advanced to the center of the field to meet him. He is however alone in his profound dejection. Even his hands are wrapped in his isolating mantle. His dog, about to greet him joyfully, arrests his leap as he senses trouble. The shepherds respect his despair, holding back discreetly; and whereas one of them does stare at him, the other diminishes this impudence by looking directly past him towards us, sympathetically, as though we had all witnessed a disaster. His glance is a barrier that maintains the privacy of Joachim's sorrow. (When, in another fresco, Joachim and Anna embrace joyfully at the gate after learning that they are to have a child, they are similarly insulated from approaching spectators by the stare of a strange, darkly-shrouded old woman.) In Assisi, the saint and the beggar look intently at each other; yet here Joachim and the two shepherds, despite their overt separation, seem no less united in a common experience. They are enfolded by a sensitive rock, and their thoughts are, as it were, joined by the lighted plane that flows quietly behind their heads. Much more than Assisi, this is a drama of the mind.

Such exalted drama culminates, of course, in the figures and the faces, but it is formed, we have seen, by the tense, seemingly inevita-

6

ble order of the entire field. In the scene of the *Cloak*, on the other hand, while the head and shoulders of the saint are firmly set in the landscape, the lower part of his body, and all of the pauper, might, it seems, be readily shifted to one side or another. None of the rocks braces the pauper's forward inclination; there is only a counter-movement of the hillock at the right that, taking off from the man's back at an indecisive point, leaves him more than ever detached. In the Arena Chapel by contrast the figures are almost like Gothic cathedral statues (Fig. 19), uniform with the wall—here natural—of rock.

The shallow but vivid space in the Paduan fresco is measured inward left and right, and at the same time fenced, by Joachim and the shed. They are turned at corresponding angles. Between them the shepherds create a chiastic pattern, the one nearer Joachim placed at the angle of the shed, the one nearer the shed at the angle of Joachim. This firm but rhythmical order of verticals—the woof we might say—is interwoven with freer horizontal strands, all beginning or ending in the head of Joachim. One unites, as we have mentioned, the three heads and continues into the towering crag at the far right. Another flows upward from the old man's halo along the crowns of the trees, and a third courses downward from him through the dog and sheep, or vice versa. As Rintelen has shown, such multiple horizontal movements are evident in many compositions in the Arena Chapel—the *Nativity*, for instance, the *Birth of the Virgin*, or the *Raising of Lazarus* (Fig. 17).

The principle of design of the *Legend* is again different (Fig. 15). The single forms are voluminous, but they are united more by lines in one plane. They do not engender broad compositional rhythms. Indeed, alongside the Arena frescoes those in Assisi seem static, and sometimes hierarchic. It might be said that these qualities in the *Gift of the Cloak* originate in its position as the central composition in a bay containing three. But when Giotto designs a fresco just below a transverse arch at the center of an entire wall of the Arena Chapel he accents the middle by means of a ciborium without diminishing the fluid, dynamic interrelationship of the figures (Fig. 18).

7

A judgment of the relationship of the frescoes in Assisi and Padua is bound of course to involve values. This indeed is the only point at which almost all students unite: in the belief that Padua consistently manifests the greater art. Now a full awareness of this qualitative difference has forced many of the proponents of the *Legend* in the last ten years (Bauch, Brandi, Longhi, Oertel, Toesca, to name only a few) to take a new position. They hold that the need for rapid completion of the cycle, which can be inferred from the stylistic differences within it, limited Giotto's role for the most part to compositional designs. He presumably drew these designs on the plaster, while assistants undertook the painting itself.

This view does not seem to me to reduce the stylistic difficulties in the slightest. As my brief analysis of the frescoes was intended to demonstrate, the compositional differences between the two cycles are profound. Indeed I can more easily imagine the master of the Arena Chapel painting particular figures in the *Legend*, such as St. Francis kneeling before the seraph or supporting the church of the Lateran, than laying out the compositions of these diffuse stories. It is more conceivable—though this possibility has not been proposed —that Giotto provided for each fresco only an indication of the relationship of the two or three chief actors, in the manner of the sketches drawn in the borders of manuscripts of the time (especially French) by the *chef d'atelier* for his assistants. Even then we would have to suppose that the painters of the frescoes freely shifted in space the position of the figures indicated in the drawings. This hypothesis of an elementary sketch would reduce Giotto's role much further than has hitherto been claimed, and it would at the same time render it proportionately more elusive. How could we, with any assurance, differentiate a participation of this sort from the work of a competent follower of the master?

The differences between the frescoes in Assisi and Padua appear of course within a broad context of resemblance, but, this said, their purposes are so divergent as to be in some respects diametrically opposed. No such variation of character and strength occurs within the documented works of any other artist of the time. Nor does it occur in the painting of Giotto himself *after* the Arena Chapel, although until a few months ago this statement would have had to be qualified by the observation that few later paintings from Giotto's own brush are available for comparison. All critics are agreed that the artistic personality of the Arena Chapel pervades every aspect of the *Maestà* now in the Uffizi (Fig. 62), and perhaps also two or three other panels, but the only surviving late fresco cycles, in S. Croce, were impossible to judge, at least in any narrower sense, because in 1853 the painter Bianchi coated them with a film of tempera to make them look intact and, if I may say so, super-Giottesque. Perhaps it was the repaint that recently led one scholar, a believer in Giotto's generalship in Assisi, to deny him any role in the Bardi Chapel, although the *Stigmatization*, just outside the Chapel, which had been more or less successfully cleaned, should have served as a warning. In any event, within the Chapel during the past months this veil has been lifted, inch by inch, with exquisite care. Its removal reveals to us here and there—amidst the execution of assistants—the full glory of Giotto's late art (Figs. 20, 21). This art is broad and serene compared to the Arena Chapel. It is also, we see now, astonishingly subtle in color as well as varied and delicate in texture. In the scene of St. Francis before the Sultan, the most beautiful in the Chapel, the luminous cloth and the purplish-brown flesh of the blackamoors beneath shining white turbans suggest—*pace* Vasari!—the taste of Venice. Such qualities are announced, however, in the frescoes in the Arena Chapel, and the Bardi frescoes remain indissociable from them. (I cannot refrain from adducing the famous fresco of the Death of St. Francis, now being deprived of Signor Bianchi's benighted but skilful efforts to improve Giotto's design by adding some big gables with trimmings at the left and right sides of the fresco [Figs. 22, 23]. The reproductions show successive stages in their removal.)

The differences between Assisi and Padua are recognized, of course, not only by students who deny a common authorship but also by those who uphold it. These proponents have attempted perforce to widen as much as possible the interval of time between

9

the two cycles, pressing the *Legend* back to 1295 or even 1290, though the difficulties that so early a date entail are usually avoided by placing the beginning of the work in 1295–1300. Now the Arena Chapel (or, at least, a lost work in the same style) had, as we have shown, certainly been begun in 1304–1305. Thus no more than ten years—and very likely less—separated the execution of the *Legend* and the formation of the Paduan phase of Giotto's style. In the light of this chronological closeness one would suppose that, if the two cycles were by the same painter, it would be easy to demonstrate that the one shows an internal development towards the other. This no one has ever even *tried* to do. The truth is that if the Assisi frescoes (apart from the first) were executed in the order of the narrative, the development is in most respects *away* from Padua. Partly to surmount this obstacle some students have eliminated Giotto from almost all the thirteen later scenes on the left wall.

These, then, are some of the difficulties, as I see them, of accepting the *Legend of St. Francis* as Giotto's, and I agree with Professor Offner and a few similar die-hards that they are insuperable. But the denial in turn entails its own very serious problems. These are not simply the apparent opposition of the early sources, disquieting enough, but also considerations of what we may call general historical plausibility. In 1305, when the Arena Chapel was under way, Giotto was at least 29 years old, and more probably 39. At this age he must already have been an independent master for many years, with a long record of radical innovation. Yet in the eyes of those scholars who attribute the *Legend* to another painter, not a single work by Giotto from the pre-Paduan years has survived (the now ruinous mosaic of the *Navicella* is surely later). More disturbing still, not a single surviving painting of the period has been said to reflect his art! And though in fourteenth- and fifteenth-century writing we hear much of the revival of painting around 1300, and of the contribution of the Roman master Cavallini as well as the Florentines Cimabue and Giotto, in the eyes of our scholars the great innovations in the nave of the Upper Church of Assisi would all have been wrought by anonymous, unsung masters. We are confronted with a strongly aching void, which I propose partly to fill, though not primarily because of the ache.

For many years some scholars have attributed to Giotto both the *Legend* and, in the period just before he undertook the *Legend*, a group of frescoes in the two bays nearest the entrance of the Upper Church as well as roundels representing saints and prophets in the transept of Sta. Maria Maggiore, Rome (Fig. 73). The frescoes in the Upper Church usually included in the group are: the *Pentecost* and *Ascension* (Fig. 70) on the entrance wall; the *Lamentation* (Fig. 67) and the fragmentary *Resurrection* on the south wall of the first or entrance bay; on the north wall, the two scenes of Joseph in the first bay (Fig. 69) and the two scenes of Isaac in the second bay, on either side of the window (Figs. 24, 25); and, finally, the vault over the first bay representing the Four Doctors of the Church. The reasons for the attribution of this group of frescoes have never been adequately set forth, and the attribution has not in fact been accepted either by some other advocates of Giotto's authorship of the *Legend* or by any of those who deny the *Legend* to him.

The paintings in this group vary both in style and in quality. The two Isaac scenes and the *Lamentation*, first of all, are greatly superior to the others (Figs. 24, 25, 67). They are in fact outstanding among all the Old and New Testament scenes in the Upper Church for their advanced contruction of space, their lucid geometric design, and their vivid action. The Isaac scenes are no less exceptional in iconography and content, though this has not previously been observed. Their very subjects have in fact often been confused, not so much because of their damaged state as their narrative singularity.

It is evident that these frescoes represent two episodes in the nasty story of brotherly strife abetted by maternal self-indulgence and fraud that has, throughout history, held everyone with horrified fascination. Precisely what is happening in the two frescoes is, however, not quite so apparent. You will remember that Isaac, blind and sensing his approaching death, asked Esau, elder of his twin boys and his favorite, to prepare to receive the patriarchal blessing by bringing his father some venison. You remember too that it was not Esau but Jacob who managed to appear first at the bedside of his father, as in the fresco, bearing a bowl of cooked meat (Fig. 26). At his side, equally still and expectant, is Rebekah, who planned the ruse by which her beloved son might obtain a blessing not rightfully his. Jacob's neck and hands are covered—very modishly covered—with goatskins to simulate his brother's hairy growth. While Isaac's eyes, unseeing, are turned out toward the beholder, his left hand is extended to touch, and thus to identify, his son, and his right hand, no longer visible, very probably was raised close to his body in a gesture of benediction. Jacob wears a halo as both the spiritual successor and the material heir of his father.

The action in the second fresco follows immediately on the first (Fig. 25). Jacob—for it is undoubtedly he though little is left—stands in the doorway after the blessing, eavesdropping. Esau now offers an almost identical dish of meat and, in his right hand, a spoon, drawing closer than Jacob, no doubt because he is guiltless and aware of his father's preferential affection (Fig. 27). The striking woman near him, not shoulder to shoulder as in the preceding scene but behind and a little apart, has always been identified as Rebekah (Fig. 31). She is, however, younger and differently dressed than the figure in the first scene. Possibly she is one of Esau's wives, but, lacking evidence, we can identify her only as a woman—a very knowing woman—of the household, like the one outside St. Anne's chamber in the Arena Chapel (Fig. 63). With a beautiful movement that suggests defense and fear, she presses a pitcher (of wine, perhaps) close to her bosom.

The first of these scenes is rather frequently represented in Christian art. Despite behavior that, on the face of it, seems scarcely praiseworthy—though no doubt it appeared less reprehensible in those rugged ancient days—Jacob became the hero of the story. Once he had assumed a place in the succession of patriarchs his method of acquiring this place was subsequently explained in two different ways. Rabbinic thought, which for the present purpose concerns us little, transformed Esau into, if I may say so, a still greater scoundrel whose defeat was an absolute necessity. Marked as a sinner, we are told, by his hairy skin, Esau committed such monstrous crimes that his grandfather Abraham died of grief and his father wilfully became blind. The statement in Genesis that the youthful Esau sold his birthright only when he was nearly starved, and only at Jacob's insistence, is conveniently forgotten. Patristic and medieval theology, on the other hand, invoked the method of allegorical interpretation. What Jacob did at his mother's bidding, said St. Augustine, and after him countless others, was not a lie but a mystery. Jacob is Christ or the Church blessed by a prophet who senses, without actually seeing, the truth. Jacob's replacement of Esau foretells the replacement of the Old Testament by the New. This change is promoted by Rebekah, who really is the Holy Ghost or the Church. Even the goatskins, donned by Jacob to obtain a blessing, are proleptic symbols of the liturgical gloves of bishops worn to handle the Host and obtain grace.

The scene of Isaac blessing Jacob was included in the great Early Christian cycles of Old Testament illustrations that were painted on the nave walls of the Roman basilicas. In the mosaic in Sta. Maria Maggiore Isaac lays his right hand on the head of a diminutive son, while Rebekah—whose presence at the blessing is not mentioned by the Bible—gesticulates excitedly at the side (Fig. 34). A scene below, now ruinous, represents Esau before Isaac. In the fifth-century fresco in S. Paolo fuori le Mura, known only through a seventeenth-century copy, Jacob, propelled by his mother, hurries a bowl of meat to Isaac, who already raises a hand in blessing (Fig. 35). The scene in Old St. Peter's, likewise known only through a late drawing, was similar. The Byzantine Octateuchs carry forward this tradition, and in the essentially similar fresco of the twelfth century in S. Giovanni in Porta Latina, Rome, Rebekah stands between father and son (Fig. 36).

In Byzantine and West Medieval art the blessing is commonly combined with a proving. Jacob usually bends or kneels before his father, and in the mosaic at Monreale and in the Cappella Palatina Isaac places one hand on his son's hairy neck, another on his hairy hands (Fig. 40). This Byzantine laying on of hands becomes a more intimate embrace in Italian, and then German fourteenth-century paintings (Fig. 41). In Romanesque and Gothic art Jacob's benediction—and this is characteristic of these universalizing Christian centuries—is given in a Christian manner (Figs. 42, 43). His left hand feels Jacob's neck or hand, often grasping it as in our fresco. German painters from about 1300 on find the proof and the physical evidence so engrossing that Jacob comes to resemble less his brother than the goat itself (Fig. 43).

It is evident from this brief survey that the Assisi fresco owes the figure of a supervisory Rebekah between father and son to the Roman tradition, while the combination of blessing and proving, which appears also in Roman painting around 1300 (Fig. 38), derives from the Gothic. But there the resemblances with the past stop. Jacob does not offer Isaac food, nor does he (as described in Genesis) kneel or even approach his father. Instead he stands stock-still at a distance, a watchful, confident, almost arrogant, young man. He wears a handsome yellow mantle over a red tunic, and even the goatskins, which resemble less a hairy growth than a fine pair of fur gloves and a matching scarf, contribute to his elegance. He and his mother are firmly held in the space by the frame of dark red curtains, one of which she holds away as though they had just entered the room. Jacob and Rebekah, alike in their outlines, the position of their left arms, and the folds of their drapery, both have their eyes fixed on Isaac. The old man reaches across the interval to feel Jacob's hand, creating a unique diagonal in the design that extends up through the folds of Jacob's mantle. Even when Isaac's right hand was visible the chief center of interest must have been his proving hand in front of the bright flashing mantles and the two faces above it, tense and expectant. The benediction itself is not more prominent in the fresco than the proof of the son's identity and the progress of the deception. The painting dwells on the human situation as much as on the theological allegory, on the biblical narrative rather than its medieval exegesis. As we look at the scene the words spoken by Isaac when he touched Jacob's skin ring in our ears: "The voice is Jacob's voice, but the hands are the hands of Esau."

Unlike Jacob's appearance before his father, Esau's is very rarely represented. Even Ghiberti, who scatters in one space seven more or less significant incidents in the early lives of the twins, including at the very center Isaac presumably asking Esau to go hunting, at the far right Esau doing so, and at the left four women altogether superfluous but for their melodious posturing, does not find room for the woeful meeting (Fig. 44). It does however appear as early as the fourth century, in the ruinous mosaic in Sta. Maria Maggiore in Rome, where Isaac seems to withdraw at the unexpected visit. Sometimes he lies motionless, granting his older son no sign of recognition whatever (Fig. 45); occasionally he gives the sort of second-class benediction described in Genesis, which was later interpreted as the ultimate salvation of the Jews. In most of the portrayals Esau is rejected by Isaac, and often he grieves (Fig. 46). The now fragmentary fresco from Cavallini's cycle in Sta. Cecilia in Rome—very close in time and in style to the painting in Assisi—presents the first moments of the episode, when Isaac raises a hand—his left—in surprise and confusion (Fig. 37). Esau, bearing a bow, dangles before his father the succulent fruits of the chase, a prominent "still-life" worthy of the chief master of the *Legend of St. Francis*, who, if he had been required to paint this subject, certainly would have exploited it eagerly.

In Assisi there is none of this. Esau's bowl is almost indistinguishable from Jacob's, and indeed the painter evidently believed that the deep contrast between the two episodes would become most apparent if they were given a broad, immediately apprehended likeness. The setting is the same and the figures similar, even though to introduce a woman alongside Esau the painter had to depart from the Bible, from all later texts, and all but one earlier representation. But whereas in the first scene Isaac and Jacob are joined by a handclasp, and the figures are all locked in a timeless geometric order (Isaac is even supported), all the figures in the second fresco are engaged in

15

movements that can only be described in paradoxical terms as both sudden, impulsive, and sustained.

A shift in the mood and action of the narrative entails, as in *Joachim's Return* and other scenes in the Arena Chapel (Figs. 14, 16), a change in the location of the figures in the field. To convey the eagerness of this second appearance and its impact upon the bewildered Isaac, the figures have been shifted all the way to the left. The old man, no longer supported and turning into an unstable position, waves his arms in space. His right is very tentative, his left gropes at the very place (beautifully enough) where Jacob's hand had been (Fig. 30). The folds of the drapery swirl in response to his agitation. They create at the same time a second rhythmic movement that, exactly as in the *Return of Joachim*, courses downward from the center of the design. Esau eagerly brings his bowl close enough for Isaac to smell, his arm curved like his father's but moving above it and in the opposite direction (Fig. 27). The woman behind him presses the pitcher close to her bosom. Her movement, self-conscious and self-protective, is the more striking because its direction is opposite to Esau's though parallel to Isaac's. She gazes with a feline fixedness at the old man. His eyes, not closed as so often in medieval painting, are turned toward the beholder, while Esau looks off into the distance at the left.

These glances are so controlled and so vivid that they establish almost tangible channels across the space. Thus the drama culminates in them while, or rather because, they participate in the geometry of the design. The character of these glances is approximated in other late Dugento works, especially those of Cimabue and Duccio (Fig. 47), but this is the first post-antique painting in which sight is focussed to this degree and given so fundamental a role in the structure and content of a painting. From such a model the chief painter of the *Legend* learned to control and intensify the glances, but only in the Arena Chapel are they equally embedded in the design (Figs. 18, 59).

It is interesting that this great conquest should appear, among surviving works, in the representation of events occasioned by blindness. Only after the vivid realization of sight could sightlessness become fully meaningful. It is the passion with which the painter of the Isaac scenes sought and achieved mastery of the glance that gives to these frescoes their exceptional and altogether unforgettable poignancy.

What is happening in this unique tableau? Isaac certainly has not yet rejected Esau, nor has he blessed him, the two actions in the story which have theological significance. The painter has chosen a prior moment when, according to Genesis, "Isaac his father said unto Esau, who art thou? And Esau said I am thy son, thy first-born. And Isaac trembled very exceedingly." The three figures manifest three degrees of awareness of the larger situation: the woman knows full well what has happened and what is likely to happen next; Isaac has only the first premonitions of the deception, and Esau is totally innocent. Esau, in fact, is conceived with an extraordinary sympathy, manifested, so far as I can see, only once again in the history of art, by an artist of whom we would expect it —Rembrandt. In the fresco he has become a central figure. His mantle of sky blue is one of the two brightest colors in either scene. He is dressed more simply than Jacob, and he is hefty, but his head is noble and his countenance open, unlike the cold, crafty mask of his brother (Figs. 28, 29). While he extends the bowl and the spoon towards Isaac he does not look at him but stares straight off into the distance, and this conspicuous detachment together with the parallel curves of the arms suggests that the two will never meet. Thus, in this remarkable combination of realistic and symbolic action, Esau has become an image of innocence and perpetual frustration. Possibly a reference to the blind Hebrews is intended, but at the very least such a metaphor is heavily permeated by the literal, human content of the story. That it is this about which the painter cares most is shown also by the bold introduction, as a counterpart to Rebekah, of a wholly unprecedented woman, for she has an important role in the drama of personal relations but none whatever in the mystical allegories. The depth and subtlety of this novel content can have been achieved only by a great artist.

17

As examples of religious mysteries transformed by human—or humanist—motivation our frescoes are equalled in the period around 1300 only by Giotto's frescoes in Padua, where the progressive episodes of salvation are profoundly infused with familiar thought and emotion. During this period the reinterpretations of the traditional stories go so far as to present earthly desires of such strength that they conflict with the divine plan. In some late thirteenth-century paintings the Virgin Mary, for instance, tries passionately to keep Christ from climbing the ladder to the cross (Fig. 49), and in religious texts she even berates God for requiring the blood of her son. These accents are strongest in Franciscan writing, such as the famous *Meditations on the Life of Christ*, and it was the Franciscans, for whose main church our frescoes were painted, who advocated the emotional reliving of scripture.

The chief sources of the new art at Assisi are in Rome. Cavallini's paintings demonstrate this, although the only comparable works by him that have survived are late, and perhaps influenced by the early paintings of our own master. The Assisi paintings are especially close to the mosaic of the Birth of the Virgin in Sta. Maria in Trastevere, ca. 1291, sharing even elements of the setting such as the railing around the bed and the curtains (Fig. 52). More remarkable, a bedside attendant in the mosaic holds a pitcher in exactly the same manner as the woman alongside Esau, one hand supporting it below, the other on the handle (Fig. 31). This pitcher-bearer, ultimately perhaps antique, appears before our Dugento version in Byzantine representations of the Birth of the Virgin (Fig. 54) and later in Italian Trecento portrayals of closely related subjects (Fig. 55). The woman is evidently traditional there but not in scenes of Esau before Isaac; and even when, in the companion scene of Isaac blessing Jacob, Rebekah carries an urn, she bears it in one hand only (Fig. 40). These facts indicate that the woman in the Assisi fresco, and probably the entire composition, reflect Cavallini's mosaic in Sta. Maria in Trastevere. If this were true we would be provided with a *terminus post quem* for the fresco. We would have the first tangible indication of a precise date that has so far been advanced.

Close comparison of the women bearing pitchers in the fresco and in the mosaic reveal small but significant differences. The scarf is laid higher on the head in the fresco, disclosing much of the hair, and the articulation of the hand, the wrist and fingers is greatly superior, even allowing for the relative intractability of mosaic. In both respects the woman in the fresco recalls ancient figures; indeed her extraordinary poise as well as the beautiful movement of her hand through space seem to presuppose study of an Early Christian or an ancient model (Fig. 53). Neither a Byzantine work, however rich in Hellenic suggestions, nor a painting by Cavallini would in itself seem to suffice. The extraordinary qualities of the Assisi woman, in fact, suggest the possibility that she, rather than the pitcher-bearer in Cavallini's mosaic, may have been the original of these two closely related figures.

Cavallini's composition of the *Birth of the Virgin* consists of an equilibrium of curving, overlapping movements engendered primarily by the balanced movements of the figures. In the mosaic this kind of design is less developed than in Assisi; only in the Arena Chapel (Figs. 18, 59) or, for that matter, in Raphael or Poussin, can we find anything equally concentrated and grand. The painter of the Assisi fresco, like Cavallini, seems to have responded in this respect also to Early Christian and perhaps even to antique models. The latter were probably reliefs, especially on sarcophagi, but our master would, I suppose, have been entranced by a painting such as the *Victory of Theseus over the Minotaur* from Herculaneum, especially because of its supple figures, its eurythmy of gesture, and its intent actors, one of them extending an arm like Isaac and another rapt like pseudo-Rebekah (Fig. 57). Whether Roman paintings were known or knowable around 1290 is a moot question, but, as Professor Panofsky has pointed out to me, a drawing of another antique composition of Theseus and the Minotaur appears in an Italian manuscript dated 1467 and apparently is contemporary with it (Fig. 56). The drawing reproduces exactly the main figures in the fresco painted in the "Basilica" of Herculaneum and now in the National Museum in Naples. Since at this time the fresco, along with the entire town of Herculaneum, was deeply buried, the author of the drawing probably had access to another example of this composition.

Both ancient and late Dugento Roman paintings, though related to the Assisi frescoes, lack some of their most impressive qualities. In the fresco of Isaac and Esau the clear, rational differentiation of the action, with each figure allotted a different degree of awareness of deception, is not Roman but Giottesque and Florentine. Not Roman either is the deep relation of the figures with the painted building, the rectangle of the frame, and the architecture of the church itself. In this precise sense the Assisi figures have a structural character, like the figures in the early frescoes in the Arena Chapel. They approximate anthropomorphized shafts, and the principle is in fact nascent Florentine reinforced by French Early or High Gothic (Fig. 51). The Upper Church itself is a beautiful adaptation of French Gothic architecture.

The Assisi figures are of course Mediterranean and they retain a greater independence of their surroundings than those in the North. The architecture is adjusted to them, as subtly as possible, but if necessary at some sacrifice of narrative realism. For the sake of narrative continuity and probably also narrative contrast the building in the two frescoes is very much alike. Unlike Cavallini's house it fills almost the entire pictorial field, creating an interior of perfect dimensions for the dramatic action. It is large enough to give the action majesty and resonance, and yet not so large as to disperse it in its ambience. The space is subdivided above and below. Its upward reach is curtailed by the rods and the borders of the curtains, and its extension below is limited, at an almost exactly equivalent level, by the wall around the bed. By checking the flow of the space these partial barriers contribute to the dominance of the figures and the intensity of their action. So fundamental is this function that when Isaac is lowered a little in the second scene the height of the curtain, and even of the entire building, is dropped proportionately.

This very same measured relationship of figure, building, and pictorial field is visible in the Arena Chapel, though vertical delimitation in these frescoes is usually less urgent because the longer axis of the scenes is horizontal (Fig. 65). In the *Annunciation to St. Anne*, however, two main figures are kneeling or seated on the floor, and Giotto has introduced a low portico as well as a curtain and furniture to accomplish the same purpose (Fig. 63). The chief painter of the *Legend* however has little conception of structure and proportionate relationships between figure and setting (Fig. 64).

It is a crucial fact that, while the frescoes of the *Legend* have a vertical format exactly like the Isaac scenes, the space above and below the figures is not fenced in in the same manner, and a comparable sense of measure is lacking in every respect. The scenes have busy, elaborate heights, either buildings (Figs. 64, 66) or landscapes (Fig. 15). What, in other words, the Isaac Master (as well as the painter of the Arena Chapel) wanted to do and knew how to do, the painter of the *Legend* did not do—did not *want* to or *could* not do, even with the Isaac scenes before his eyes.

No matter what pictorial qualities we consider, the pattern of relationship of the Isaac scenes, the *Legend*, and the Arena Chapel remains essentially the same. The telling pantomime of the Isaac scenes, motivated by deep thought and feeling, is, we have observed, visible everywhere in the Chapel (Figs. 18, 59). In neither of these works is there any trace of the more tentative, rather petty gestures often apparent in the *Legend*, such as a pointing thumb, or fingers to lips or cheek, or chin in hand (Fig. 58). And even where in the *Legend* the gestures resemble those in the Isaac scenes (which they reflect) their strength is dissipated by their isolation in a sea of empty space or their almost Lilliputian scale amidst structures of towering stone (Figs. 64, 66).

If we draw closer to the figures, and set alongside heads from the Arena Chapel or the *Maestà* (Figs. 59, 62) those that have been selected by the supporters of the *Legend* themselves as the clearest evidence in the cycle of Giotto's own brush (Figs. 60, 61), do we not wonder how it is possible to grant to these blunt physical pres-

21

ences of Assisi the same sublime source? In the Isaac scenes however we recognize at once Giotto's exalted conception of personality and a similar radiance of mind and emotion, though the later work is more pungent and more assured (Figs. 28, 29, 32, 33). The two differ considerably of course in color and, it is evident, in touch and facture. The fine silken hair of Padua and of the *Maestà* in the Uffizi resembles only in its waviness the beautiful locks in the Isaac scenes, almost late antique in their fluency (Figs. 33, 62). Form is created more by line and by graduated modeling in these scenes, by broad planes of light and dark in Padua. But this is the kind of difference that accords with the general historical transformation of style, and in fact would, in the early work of Giotto, be predictable. The difference of mode or phase does not conceal the remarkable likeness between the head of Esau and the head of the youth in the *Raising of Lazarus* (Figs. 29, 59), or the head of Jacob with Lazarus himself (Figs. 28, 59). And, like the designs as a whole, these details disclose an artist of similar vision and—I do not hesitate to say—equal stature.

The style of the Isaac scenes derives principally from Cavallini, whose innovations were in turn based on Early Christian art, the more Hellenistic phases of Byzantine, and perhaps the antique itself. The Isaac scenes themselves reflect a direct experience of these earlier arts. The scenes were deeply influenced also by the linear vitality and the drama of Cimabue, so that they blend the two dominant —and quite diverse—pictorial trends in the late Dugento. The debt to Cimabue is especially obvious in the flashing drapery of Jacob and Rebekah (Figs. 26, 47). The two scenes owe something also, as we have seen, to French Gothic sculpture; indeed they disclose the impact of Gothic not only in their forms but also, as we have observed, in their iconography. This connection with the North has its significance for the problem of authorship, because scholars have already discerned an assimilation of French Gothic sculpture in the frescoes of the Arena Chapel. On the whole, however, the Isaac scenes are more classical, the Arena Chapel more Gothic. This sequence corresponds to the broad trend of the time. Giotto would have himself encompassed the development from Nicola Pisano to Giovanni, and the evolution of Tuscan painting would parallel that of sculpture.

The frescoes in the first bay of the Upper Church, on the vault over it and on the adjoining entrance wall are commonly grouped with the Isaac scenes, but, despite their obvious connections with the scenes, they are rather diverse in style. Closest to the Isaac scenes is the *Lamentation* on the opposite wall, which was certainly designed, and probably executed, at least in part, by the same painter (Fig. 67). Its composition, as often noticed, bears a fundamental resemblance to the same subject in Padua (Fig. 68). The ascending Christ in the adjoining fresco on the entrance wall is strikingly similar to the corresponding figure in the Arena Chapel (Figs. 70, 71). The Paduan *Hope* derives from the same pattern (Fig. 72). The execution of the Assisi *Ascension* is, however, perfunctory, and even the figure of Christ, though more impressive than the apostles below, does not attain the strength of the Isaac scenes. But its origin certainly lies there—compare the beautiful hands with Isaac's or pseudo-Rebekah's. The frescoes of the four Doctors of the Church in the vault, while deriving likewise from the style of the Isaac Master, draw away from it towards the *Legend*. Indeed the qualities of the vault, especially of the figure of St. Augustine, reappear in the *Legend*, at the extreme left and right, for instance, in the *Ordeal by Fire* (Fig. 66) and at the far right in the *Award of the Rules*. Other frescoes in the last bay, such as the *Discovery of the Silver Cup in Benjamin's Sack*, though related to the Isaac scenes, disclose also, most conspicuously in the elaborate architecture, the emergence of the taste (though not clearly the hand) of the chief master of the *Legend* (Fig. 69). Here then we can see the diversity of the two styles in works produced at the same time!

I can scarcely begin to draw the implications of the position I have outlined this evening. It is in accord with our earliest written source, the chronicler who between 1312 and 1318 said that Giotto painted in the church of S. Francesco at Assisi. Inasmuch as the Isaac scenes were painted some years earlier than the *Legend* they con-

23

form more perfectly to the old tradition, first explicitly recorded by Antonio Billi in 1510, that Giotto *began* to acquire fame by painting in the church of S. Francesco, Assisi. This tradition has a claim to authenticity precisely because it conveys a kind of fact that is normally so little regarded at the time. In this connection we must note, too, that Riccobaldo, when listing Giotto's works, did not adopt an alphabetical order but placed Assisi first, before *Ariminum* and Padua.

If the *Legend of St. Francis* is by a follower of Giotto, then the attribution of the cycle to Giotto himself by both Ghiberti and Vasari would not be very surprising, for both attribute to the master works that are actually only by followers. Inasmuch as the Isaac scenes are earlier than the *Legend*, they allow a longer, and therefore a more proper and a more credible period for the transformation of Giotto's style into the Paduan phase. Within that interval there is one important work that seems to me closely related to the style of the scenes: the beautiful crucifix in Sta. Maria Novella in Florence. In it the head of St. John (retouched here and there), his crown of hair, and his drapery resemble the figure of Esau (Fig. 75). It is significant that this seems to be the crucifix which a document of 1312 identifies as a work of Giotto. It may have been painted in the late nineties by an excellent, rather independent assistant in his shop.

Long before this some historian will have asked, why did Giotto not receive the commission for the *Legend* if he had demonstrated his mastery in the Upper Church just before the cycle was undertaken? Perhaps the general of the order disliked Giotto's personality, or Giotto the remuneration. Perhaps the painter was knocked down again by the pig that bowled him over in Sacchetti's story, and this time badly broke his arm.

How am I now to formulate my conclusion about this complex and difficult matter? We must accept the fact that the great problems in the realm of style about which conviction was more readily attainable were solved years ago. It is our task today to try to get on with the more abstruse. Confirmation of our reconstruction by Morellian method may be unobtainable, but who would deny that the larger aspects of design and content, when identified and defined precisely, are less telling, especially when the authorship of a great new art is at stake?

The numerous scholars who have admitted the Isaac scenes to Giotto's *oeuvre* have admitted a Trojan horse. The scenes exhibit so many fundamental qualities of the Arena Chapel that are conspicuously absent from the *Legend* that they serve to eliminate Giotto as the designer of the *Legend* with the certainty almost of a mathematical equation. The Isaac scenes enable us to shake off the more readily not only the *Legend* but such lesser barnacles that have encrusted Giotto's *oeuvre* as the fresco in the Lateran of *Boniface VIII Proclaiming the Jubilee of 1300* (Fig. 74).

Our proposed reconstruction of the early work of Giotto is not free of problems. Its least satisfactory consequence is the anonymity of the *Legend of St. Francis*, and its most troublesome aspect is the lack of paintings by Giotto documenting the transition from the Isaac scenes to the Arena Chapel. Where a choice must be made, however, I certainly prefer historical lacunae, conceivably remediable, to present contradictions of style, forever irreconcilable. Of one thing there can be no doubt whatever: if the Isaac Master is not Giotto, then he and not Giotto is the founder of modern painting.

References

GIOTTO AND ASSISI

BAUCH, K., "Die geschichtliche Bedeutung von Giottos Frühstil," in *Mitteilungen des Kunsthistorisches Institut in Florenz*, VII, 1953, pp. 43 ff.

BRANDI, C., "Giotto Recuperato a San Giovanni Laterno," in *Scritti di storia dell'arte in onore di Lionello Venturi*, Rome, 1956, I, pp. 55–85.

FISHER, R., "Assisi, Padua and the Boy in the Tree," *Art Bulletin*, XXXVIII, 1956, pp. 47–52.

GNUDI, C., *Giotto*, Milan, 1958 (accessible after the present book went to press).

LONGHI, R., in *Proporzioni*, II, 1948, pp. 49–51.

MEISS, M., "Reflections of Assisi: A Tabernacle and the Cesi Master," in *Miscellanea in onore di Mario Salmi* (in press).

OERTEL, R., *Die Frühzeit der Italienischen Malerei*, Stuttgart, 1953, pp. 62–76.

OFFNER, R., "Giotto, non-Giotto," in *Burlington Magazine*, LXXIV, 1939, pp. 259–268; LXXV, 1939, pp. 96–113.

SCHÖNE, W., "Studien zur Oberkirche von Assisi," in *Festschrift Kurt Bauch, Kunstgeschichtliche Beiträge zum 25. November 1957*, (n.d.) pp. 50–116.

TOESCA, P., *Gli affreschi del Vecchio e del Nuovo Testamento nella chiesa superiore del santuario di Assisi* (Artis monumenta photographice edita, IV), 3 vols., Florence, 1948.

WHITE, J., "The Date of 'The Legend of St. Francis' at Assisi," in *Burlington Magazine*, XCVIII, 1956, pp. 344 ff.

ISAAC, JACOB AND ESAU. *The Religious Sources.*

Genesis, XXVII.

Malachi, I, 2–4.

Paul, Romans, IX, 10–16; XI, 26–29.

Encyclopedia Judaica.

Universal Jewish Encyclopedia.

Ginzberg, L., *The Legends of the Jews*, 1909, I, pp. 328–340.

ST. AMBROSE, *De Isaac et Anima*, in Migne, *Patrologia Latina*, XIV, col. 527 ff.

ST. AUGUSTINE, *Against Lying*, in *Treatises on Various Subjects* (trans. by R. J. Deferrari, New York, 1952, pp. 152–155).

———, *City of God*, Bk. XVI, chap. 38.

———, *Opera Omnia*, Paris, 1837, V, pp. 19–35 (sermo IV).

ISIDORE OF SEVILLE, *Quaestiones in Veterum Testamentum*, in Migne, *op. cit.*, LXXXIII, cols. 255–258.

WALAFRID STRABO, *Glossa Ordinaria*, *ibid.*, CXIII, cols. 151–153.

ST. BONAVENTURE, *Opera Omnia*, Florence, 1882, VI, p. 453.

ISAAC, JACOB AND ESAU. *Some representations not reproduced.*

Fourth century, Sarcophagus, Paris, Louvre. J. Wilpert, *I Sarcofagi cristiani antichi*, Rome, 1929, I, pl. CXVI (1).

Drawing by Grimaldi after Early Christian fresco in old St. Peter's, Rome. J. Wilpert, *Die römischen Mosaiken und Malereien*, Freiburg i/B, 1916, I, pt. 1, fig. 121.

Byzantine, 12th century, Palermo, Cappella Palatina. O. Demus, *The Mosaics of Norman Sicily*, London, 1949, pl. 35B.

Byzantine, 12th century, Rome, Vatican Library, ms. gr. 746. J. Wilpert, *op. cit.*, p. 434, fig. 152.

English, late 12th century, Paris, Bibliothèque nationale, ms. lat. 8846, f. 1, v. *Psautier illustré (XIIIe siècle)*, Paris (Bibliothèque nationale), n.d., pl. II.

English, 14th century, British Museum Egerton 1894, f. 15. M. R. James, *Illustrations of the Book of Genesis*, Oxford, 1921, figs. 103–104.

French, 13th century, *Bible moralisée*, Oxford, Bodleian Library, ms. Auct. B. IV. 6, f. 17 v. A. de Laborde, *La Bible Moralisée*, Paris, 1911, I, pl. 17.

Bohemian, ca. 1250, New York, Morgan Library, ms. 739, f. 12. M. Harrsen, *Cursus Sanctae Mariae*, New York, 1937, pl. 7.

German, late 13th century, Zurich, Zentralbibliothek, ms. Rheinau 15, f. 37. K. Escher, *Die Bilderhandschrift der Weltchronik des Rudolf von Ems in der Zentralbibliothek Zürich*, Zurich, 1935, pl. II.

Bolognese, 14th century, Pomposa, Abbey. M. Salmi, *L'Abbazia di Pomposa*, Rome, 1936, fig. 337.

GIUSTO DE' MENABUOI, Padua, Baptistry. S. Bettini, *Giusto de' Menabuoi*, Padua, 1944, pl. 80.

MEISTER BERTRAM, Altarpiece, Hamburg, Kunsthalle. A. Dorner, *Meister Bertram*, Berlin, 1937, pl. I.

REMBRANDT, New York, Wildenstein & Co. (formerly Earl Brownlow). W. Bode, *Rembrandt*, Paris, 1899, III, pl. 217.

———, Vienna, market, a drawing. O. Benesch, *The Drawings of Rembrandt*, London, VI, 1955, pl. 1624.

A NOTE ON THE FIGURES

The dates appearing *after* many of the captions are those ascertained by the text. It has seemed more useful to record the precise limits rather than the author's estimate of the most probable date within these limits.

1. Giuliano da Rimini, 1307, *St. Francis* (detail of a retable). Gardner Museum, Boston
2. Italian 14th century, *Saint* (detail of a drawing). Fogg Museum, Cambridge
3. Follower of Giotto (pre-Paduan phase), *St. Francis*. S. Francesco, Assisi. Before 1307
4. *St. Victurinus* (retouched). St. Nicholas Chapel, S. Francesco, Assisi. Before 1307

[5]

[6]

5. Giotto, *Faith*. Arena Chapel, Padua. Probably before 1306–7
6. Giuliano da Rimini, 1307, *St. Clare* (detail). Gardner Museum, Boston

7. Follower of Giotto (Paduan phase), *Sts. Clare and Catherine*. St. Nicholas Chapel,
S. Francesco, Assisi. Before 1307

8. Giuliano da Rimini, 1307, *Madonna* (detail). Gardner Museum, Boston
9. Follower of Giotto, *Madonna and two saints*. St. Nicholas Chapel, S. Francesco, Assisi. Before 1307

10. The Cesi Master, 1308, Altarpiece. Sta. Maria, Cesi
11. Follower of Giotto, *Madonna* (detail of *Obsequies*). S. Francesco, Assisi. Before 1308
12. Follower of Giotto, *An Apostle*. St. Nicholas Chapel, S. Francesco, Assisi. Before 1308
13. Follower of Giotto, *An Apostle*. St. Nicholas Chapel, S. Francesco, Assisi. Before 1308

14. Giotto, *Joachim returning to his sheepfold*. Arena Chapel, Padua. Probably 1304–5

15. Follower of Giotto, *St. Francis giving his cloak to a poor knight.* S. Francesco, Assisi. Before 1307

[16]

[17]

16. Giotto, *Expulsion of Joachim*. Arena Chapel, Padua. Probably 1304–5
17. Giotto, *Raising of Lazarus*. Arena Chapel, Padua

[18]

18. Giotto, *Presentation in the temple.*
Arena Chapel, Padua
19. *Annunciation,* ca. 1225. West façade,
right door, Cathedral, Amiens

[19]

20. Giotto, detail of *St. Francis before the sultan*. Bardi Chapel, S. Croce, Florence
(repaint partly removed)

21. Giotto, *The Sultan* (detail). Bardi Chapel, S. Croce, Florence (after cleaning)

22. Giotto and assistants, *Death of St. Francis* (detail). Bardi Chapel, S. Croce, Florence (repaint partly removed)

23. Detail of Fig. 22 after further removal of repaint of 1853

24. Giotto (?), *Jacob and Rebekah before Isaac*. S. Francesco, Assisi. Probably just after 1291

[25]

25. Giotto (?), *Esau seeking Isaac's blessing*. S. Francesco, Assisi. Probably just after
1291

26. Giotto (?), *Jacob and Rebekah* (detail of Fig. 24)

27. Giotto (?), *Esau* (detail of Fig. 25)

28. Giotto (?), *Jacob* (detail of Fig. 24)

29. Giotto (?), *Esau* (detail of Fig. 25)

30. Giotto (?), *Isaac* (detail of Fig. 25)

31. Giotto (?), *An Attendant* (detail of Fig. 25)

[32]

32. Giotto (?), *Isaac* (detail of Fig. 25)

33. Giotto (?), *An Attendant* (detail of Fig. 25)

[34]

[35]   [36]

34. *Isaac blessing Jacob*, 432–40. Sta. Maria Maggiore, Rome.
35. 17th-century drawing after 5th-century fresco of Isaac blessing Jacob in S. Paolo fuori le mura, Rome
36. 12th century, *Isaac blessing Jacob*. S. Giovanni in Porta Latina, Rome

[37]

[38]　　　　　　　　　　　　　　　　[39]

37. Assistant of Cavallini, ca. 1293, *Esau seeking Isaac's blessing*. Sta. Cecilia, Rome
38. Roman, ca. 1295, *Isaac blessing Jacob*. Sta. Maria in Vescovio
39. Roman, ca. 1295, *Esau seeking Isaac's blessing*. Sta. Maria in Vescovio

40. Byzantine, 12th century, *Isaac blessing Jacob*. Cathedral, Monreale
41. Niccolo di Tommaso, *Isaac blessing Jacob*. Palazzo del Te, Pistoia
42. English, early 14th century, Queen Mary's Psalter, *Isaac blessing Jacob*, and *Esau seeking the blessing*. British Museum, Royal 2 B VII, f.13v.
43. German, ca. 1290, *Isaac blessing Jacob* and *Esau hunting and seeking the blessing*. Stadtbibliothek, St. Gall, MS 302, f.21v.

[44]

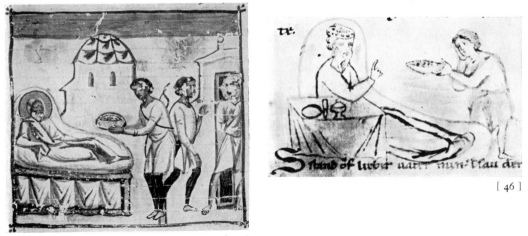

[46]

[45]

44. Ghiberti, *Story of Isaac, Jacob and Esau* (detail of doors). Baptistry, Florence
45. Byzantine, 12th century, *Esau seeking Isaac's blessing*. Biblioteca Vaticana, Vat. grec. 747, f.49
46. German, 12th century, *Esau rejected by Isaac*. Klagenfurt, Landesmuseum, VI.19, f.36

[47]

[48]

[49]

47. Cimabue, *A Prophet* (detail of *Maestà*). Uffizi, Florence
48. Cavallini, ca. 1293, *An Apostle* (detail of *Last Judgment*). Sta. Cecilia, Rome
49. Guido da Siena, *Christ mounting the cross*. Archiepiscopal Museum, Utrecht

50. Giotto, *Annunciation to Joachim*. Arena Chapel, Padua. Probably 1304–5
51. French, ca. 1240, *Job and the Devil*. North transept, central portal, Cathedral, Reims

52. Cavallini, 1291, *Birth of the Virgin*. Sta. Maria in Trastevere, Rome

[53]

[54]

[55]

[56]

53. Roman, 1st century, *Eumachia*. National Museum, Naples
54. Byzantine, 1164, *Woman holding jug* (detail of *Birth of the Virgin*). Church, Nerezi
55. Andrea Pisano, *Woman holding jug* (detail of *Birth of the Baptist*). Doors, Baptistry, Florence
56. Italian, 1467 (?), Drawing after a Roman painting of *Theseus and the Minotaur*. Servius MS, formerly W. Hiersemann, Leipzig

57. Pompeian, 1st century, *Theseus and the Minotaur*. National Museum, Naples

[58]

58. Follower of Giotto, *St. Francis preaching before the Pope*. S. Francesco, Assisi.
Before 1307–8

59. Giotto, *The Raising of Lazarus* (detail). Arena Chapel, Padua.

60. Follower of Giotto, *Pope Innocent III* (detail of *Confirmation of Rules*). S. Francesco, Assisi. Before 1307–8

61. Follower of Giotto, *St. Francis* (detail of *Gift of cloak*). S. Francesco, Assisi. Before 1307–8

62. Giotto, *Christ* (detail of *Maestà*). Uffizi, Florence

63. Giotto, *Annunciation to St. Anne*. Arena Chapel, Padua. Probably 1304–5

64. Follower of Giotto, *Vision of the fiery chariot*. S. Francesco, Assisi. Before 1307–8

65. Giotto, *Christ before the high priest*. Arena Chapel, Padua.

66. Follower of Giotto, *St. Francis before the sultan*. S. Francesco, Assisi. Before 1307–8

[67]

[68]

67. Giotto and Assistant (?), *Lamentation*. S. Francesco, Assisi
68. Giotto, *Lamentation*. Arena Chapel, Padua

[69]

69. Circle of Giotto (?), *Finding of the silver cup*. S. Francesco, Assisi

70. Assistant of Giotto (?), *Christ* (detail of *Ascension*). S. Francesco, Assisi

| 71 | [72]

71. Giotto and Assistant, *Christ* (detail of *Ascension*). Arena Chapel, Padua
72. Giotto, *Hope*. Arena Chapel, Padua

73. Roman painter (influenced by Giotto?), *Prophet*. Sta. Maria Maggiore, Rome. Ca. 1295

74. Roman painter, 1300–1301, *Boniface* VIII *proclaiming the Jubilee.* S. Giovanni in Laterano, Rome

75. Assistant of Giotto (?), *St. John* (detail of Crucifix). Sta. Maria Novella, Florence